Kittens in Japan

Atsuki Sumida

KODANSHA INTERNATIONAL
Tokyo • New York • London

Kittens in Japan

The author and publisher would like to thank the following for their assistance and support in completing this project: Arai Ryokan; Yakatabune Tsurishin; Naniwaya Sohonten; Osome; Musashiya Hozan.

Distributed in the United States by Kodansha America, Inc., 114 Fifth Avenue, New York, N.Y. 10011, and in the United Kingdom and continental Europe by Kodansha Europe Ltd., Gillingham House, 38-44 Gillingham Street, London SW1V 1HU. Published by Kodansha International Ltd., 17-14 Otowa 1-chome, Bunkyo-ku, Tokyo 112, and Kodansha America, Inc.

ISBN 4-7700-1672-7

Japan's super-fast Shinkansen, or Bullet Train, zooms at speeds of over 200 kilometers an hour.

Tokyo, originally called Edo, took its name, meaning Eastern
Capital, after the Meiji Restoration of 1868. Its population today
is about twelve million.

Perhaps the most famous train station in Japan, Tokyo Station
was completed in 1914. Its design is said to be based on that
of the station building in Amsterdam.

The *hagoita*, originally used as a kind of badminton racquet, features elaborate paintings of celebrities. Sold at temples before the New Year, they are often used as decorations in the home.

The familiar *bangasa* is a colorful umbrella traditionally made by splitting a bamboo stalk into ribs, then attaching brightly dyed paper.

The Doll Festival, held annually on March 3, features displays of elaborately dressed dolls, representing members of the ancient Imperial Court.

Beautiful and delicious Japanese sweets are traditionally enjoyed with astringent green tea. They vary in color, shape, and ingredients with the seasons.

Traditional Japanese balloons are made from sheets of brightly colored
paper, and inflated through a small hole.

The smiling mask of Okame, bringer of good fortune, and that of Hyottoko, always blowing out a flame, are often used in traditional celebrations.

Traditional small chests, adorned with brightly colored paper, are used for storing accessories worn with a kimono.

The goldfish was originally introduced into Japan from China early in the sixteenth century.

Watermelon is as much a summer favorite in Japan as in the rest of the world.

Flower cards are both beautiful and fun to play with.
Players try to match them.

Origami, or Japanese paper folding, often features animals and birds, like the crane.

While baskets are made of a variety of materials, Japanese baskets have traditionally been made of bamboo.

23

Wooden tops were once favorite children's toys, but have lost popularity in recent years. Most tops today are examples of folk handicraft, like the ones shown here.

Tokyo's futuristic Metropolitan Government Office building, completed in 1991, features a panoramic view of the city from the 45th floor.

The streets of some of Tokyo's busiest shopping and entertainment districts are often closed to traffic on Sundays and national holidays—creating what the Japanese call Pedestrian Paradise.

Tokyo Dome, popularly known as the Big Egg, is the home of the Yomiuri Giants baseball team, as well as many entertainment events and exhibitions.

As in days of old, traditional covered party boats still cruise on the rivers of Tokyo and Osaka. Inside, revelers gather around tables on tatami mat floors to eat, drink, sing, and relax.

Tempura, deep fried fish and vegetables dipped into a light sauce, was introduced into Japan from Portugal in the late sixteeth century.

Buckwheat noodles, known as soba, are delicious dipped into a cold sauce, or eaten with hot broth and garnishes.

In simpler days, when earthen cooking stoves like this one were used in most households, a wide round fan kept the coals burning brightly.

Shinobazu Pond, in Tokyo's Ueno Park, is renowned for its lush summer lotus plants, which provide shelter for migrating birds.

Ringing the bronze bell in a Japanese Buddhist temple is reputed to bring those who hear it closer to paradise.

The artistic rendering of Japanese characters ranks with literature and painting at the pinnacle of Japanese cultural tradition.

The hibachi, or charcoal brazier, was once the typical source of heat in a Japanese home.

Shiny wooden corridors are a notable feature of traditional Japanese houses.

Sliding paper doors have been used in Japanese houses
since the eighth century, and are still found in traditional-
style houses today.

Specially bred ornamental carp, called *nishikigoi*, are often found in Japanese garden ponds.

Traditional tile roofs are not only waterproof and fireproof, but they stay cool in the daytime and warm at night.

Wooden clogs, or *geta*, are still used in Japan when wearing traditional clothes.

Hanging wind-chimes, generally made of glass, ceramics, or metal, are often to be found in homes during hot weather. Their gentle tinkling seems to cool the air.

Bunraku, or puppet drama, ranks with *noh* and *kabuki* as one of Japan' three traditional dramatic art forms. It takes three puppeteers to manipulate one *bunraku* puppet.

Round, red, papier-mache *daru-ma* dolls are familiar good luck symbols, because they bounce back if struck. It's customary to fill in one of the eyes and make a wish—if it comes true, you fill in the other eye.

The traditional *jinrikisha*, or manpowered car, was once a common form of transportation. Today it can still be seen occasionally in tourist resorts and the *geisha* districts of central Tokyo.

Kabuki drama dates back almost four centuries. Its main theater in Tokyo, the *Kabuki-za*, is located in the Ginza district.

The classic Japanese kimono, one of the most elegant national costumes in the world, is still worn by women young and old on special occasions. Its classic style, almost unchanged over the years, features a gorgeously embroidered *obi* sash.

Portable shrines, called *mikoshi*, are used to carry deities though the streets during local festivals throughout Japan.

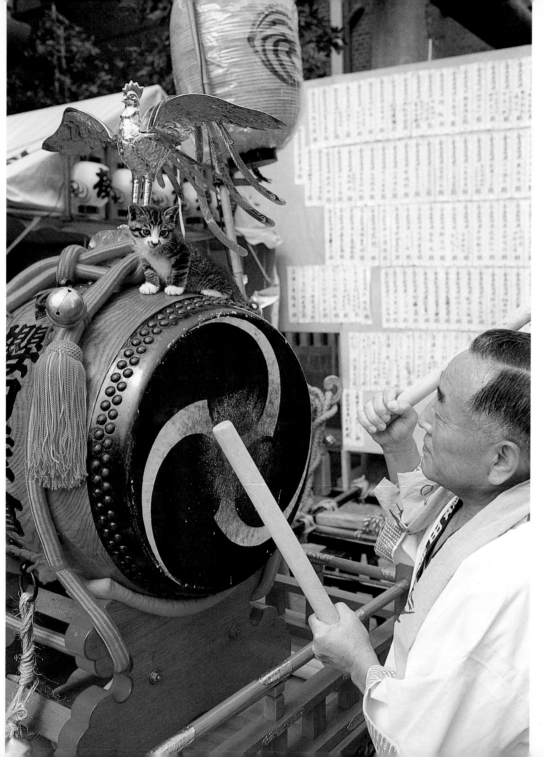

The traditional Japanese drum is beaten from a wooden float during local festivals.

53

Decorated with folded pieces of paper and thin printed stripes, these envelopes are used to hold cash gifts presented on festive occasions.

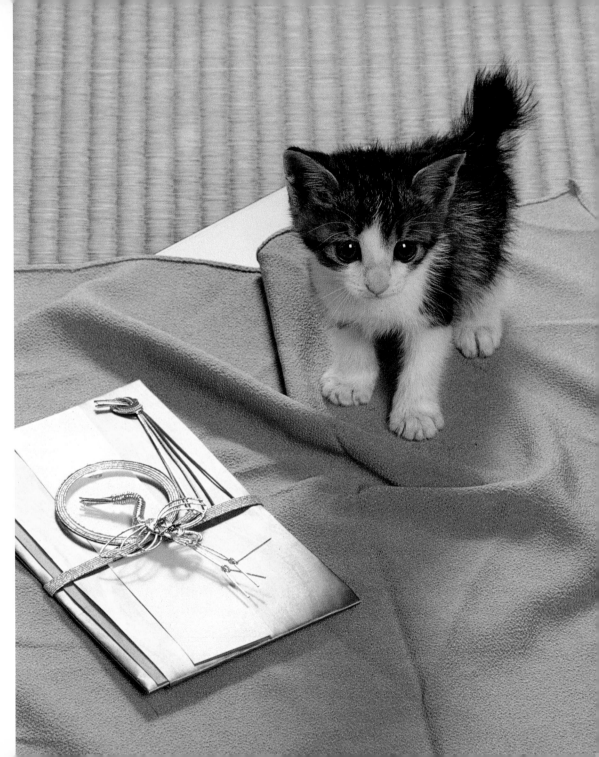

Religious amulets, purchased at temples or shrines, are carried to insure good fortune.

Sake, brewed from fermented rice and water, is usually served in ceramic flasks and tiny cups.

Noren are short, split curtains that are hung at the entrance of a Japanese shop or restaurant to indicate that it is open for business.

Casks of Japanese rice wine, or sake, are tratitional gifts at celebrations.

The approach to a Shinto shrine is marked by at least one sacred gate, or *torii*. Passing through the gate is supposed to purify visitors to the shrine.

This bamboo rake, reputed to help its owner gather in wealth, can be purchased at Tokyo's Ohtori Shrine every November.

The beckoning cat, often seen in Japanese storefronts, is thought to wave in customers.

Tai Yaki (grilled hot cakes filled with sweet bean jam) are shaped like a good luck fish, the *tai* (sea bream), which is reputed to bring happiness (*medetai*).

Grasses and reeds are especially grown in Japan as materials for constructing thatched roofs for traditional farmhouses.

The more than a thousand different types of bamboo in Japan are used for everything from construction, to utensils, to food.

Volcanic hot springs are to be found throughout Japan, attracting visitors from far and wide for their healthful benefits.

Temari, or hand ball, was used in games among court nobles during the Heian Period a thousand years ago. Decorated with colorful silk thread, it is most often used today as an ornament.

Cute dolls in traditional dress are still favorite playthings for little girls in Japan.